A Child's Book of
MYTHS and
ENCHANTING TALES

Illustrations by
MARGARET EVANS PRICE

A Classic Collection of Myth and Enchantment

For children of all ages.

These stories are reprinted from *A Child's Book of Myths*, 1934,
and *Enchantment Tales for Children*, 1926.

A CHILD'S BOOK OF MYTHS AND ENCHANTING TALES
A Classic Collection of Myth and Enchantment
Published in 2007 by Creative Edge
Copyright © 2007 Dalmatian Press, LLC

All rights reserved
Printed in China

The CREATIVE EDGE name is a trademark
of Dalmatian Press, LLC, Franklin, Tennessee 37067.
No part of this book may be reproduced or copied in any form
without the written permission of Dalmatian Press.

ISBN: 1-40378-099-4
CE10455-1106

07 08 09 CCP 10 9 8 7 6 5 4 3 2 1

THE CONTENTS

PROMETHEUS AND THE FIRE OF THE GODS

P rometheus and Epimetheus were Titans, who lived on the earth before men were created. The Titans were large and strong and could do many wonderful things.

Prometheus knew that the first men were soon coming to live on earth, and he spent most of his time, like a great father, making things ready for their coming. He planted the first seeds of fruit trees and of flowers. He opened up tiny springs on the sides of the mountains so that little streams might come running down and water the valleys. He watched over the animals and taught his brother, Epimetheus, how to help him.

To each bird and animal, Epimetheus gave a gift that would make it more useful or more beautiful. He gave wool to the sheep, and soft fur to many small animals so that man might have clothing. He gave milk to the cow, and speed to the horse, strength to the elephant, whalebone to the whale, beautiful feathers to the ostrich, and sweet songs to the birds—all things that mankind has ever since found pleasant and useful.

Last of all he decided to have ready some especially splendid gift for man himself. Prometheus tried to think of something great and beautiful enough and at last he remembered the fire of the gods.

"If," thought he, "I could go up to the sun and light a torch, perhaps I could bring fire to earth for man to use."

To each bird and animal Epimetheus gave a gift

So he climbed to the top of Mount Olympus, the home of the gods. Its tall peaks reached up into the sky, so steep that only a god or a Titan might ascend. From the very highest point Prometheus stepped off among the clouds. Then, walking carefully from one fleecy island to another, he approached the chariot of the sun as it sped across the sky, driven by Apollo and drawn by the four horses of the Day.

No man could have endured the heat from the chariot as it drew near, but Prometheus was a Titan. Stretching toward the chariot a long torch, he held it tightly as it caught fire, although the light blinded him and the fire burned his hands. Apollo passed on his way, never guessing that Prometheus had stolen some of the heavenly fire.

Hiding his torch, Prometheus hurried down the mountain of the gods until he reached the earth. There he kindled a fire among the rocks and bade Epimetheus watch it, so that it might never die out.

When man was born on earth, he used the fire to warm himself, cook his food, and to frighten away the fiercest of the animals when they prowled too near at night. He learned to use fire to bake his clay dishes so that they would hold water, and to melt gold from the rocks.

But Jupiter, the king of the gods, was angry with Prometheus for daring to steal fire from the sun, and just when man had learned to enjoy the gift of Prometheus, the god snatched it away. He forbade Prometheus ever again to approach the sun.

For a long time Prometheus considered how he might regain fire for man, who was now miserable indeed, for he had no way of cooking his food or of warming himself.

Prometheus again set out for Mount Olympus, but this time he visited Vulcan's workshop, and took some fire from his forge. He hid the stolen flame in a hollow reed so that the gods might not see it, and hurried back to earth.

Jupiter chained Prometheus to a rock on Mount Caucasus

Jupiter, looking down from Olympus, saw smoke again ascending from the earth. He was so angry that he dropped his thunderbolts, raged down from the mountain, and ordered Prometheus to put out the fires.

Prometheus refused. So Jupiter chained him to a rock on Mount Caucasus and tormented him.

PANDORA'S BOX

After Prometheus had been taken away and chained, Epimetheus was very lonely. Men loved him, just as boys love their father, and came to him for help in everything. But Epimetheus wanted someone to live with him and cheer him, because he often became sad, remembering how his brother Prometheus had been bound to the rock. Even Jupiter himself began to be sorry for Epimetheus, and decided to call the gods together in council.

There was one god who wore beautiful silver sandals with white wings growing from the heels. These sandals gave him such speed that he had only to rise into the air and take one great flying leap, and in a moment's time he would be at the other side of the sky. This god's name was Mercury; sometimes he was called "The Quicksilver." He was the messenger of all the others, and Jupiter now sent him to summon the gods.

Apollo left his chariot and came quickly at Jupiter's command. Vulcan, the craftsman of Olympus, laid down his anvil and his goldsmith's tools. But he came more slowly, for he was lame and could not hurry.

This god's name was Mercury

Venus, goddess of love and beauty, with her little son Cupid, came floating through the clouds. Juno, the queen of the gods, with her peacock, took her place at Jupiter's side. Minerva, the goddess of wisdom, came also. All the deities of Olympus ranged themselves at the right and left of Jupiter's throne to consider what might be done for Epimetheus.

They decided that Epimetheus must have a companion. Mercury was sent to the earth to bring back some soft clay. In a moment he returned with it. Vulcan, the artist of the gods, then took the clay in his hands and began to form a beautiful figure, while Jupiter looked on and told him just how he thought the companion should be made. Soon Vulcan had finished modeling a lovely clay form, not quite like that of a man, but more delicate.

Now Venus touched the clay figure and it became ivory white. The waves of soft hair which Vulcan had modeled became fine gold. Jupiter breathed on the lips and life entered the form. Her blue eyes opened, and the gods, seeing her so lovely, came nearer and gave her beautiful gifts.

Apollo, who could play sweetly on the lyre, gave her the gift of music. Mercury gave her a gentle voice and the art of knowing how to speak. They named her Pandora, which means "All-Gifted."

Venus gave her a blue robe with rich embroidery, and Mercury led her down from Mount Olympus to be a comrade for Epimetheus on the earth. Pandora was delighted with the flowers, the birds, and the sweet fruits that grew around her. She played and laughed so much that Epimetheus grew happier, and forgot that he had ever been sad.

*Venus, goddess of love and beauty, with her little son Cupid,
came floating through the clouds*

With a buzz and a roar there flew out of the box a swarm of little evil-looking creatures

Now, everything would have been perfect had it not been for Pandora's curiosity. There was a chest in Epimetheus' house which he kept tied with a strong cord. When Pandora asked if she might open the chest, Epimetheus told her that Mercury had left it, that it did not belong to them, and must not be touched. But Pandora was so curious that she continued to beg and tease Epimetheus to open the chest and look inside.

"If Mercury brought it before I came," she said, "perhaps it is full of dresses and shining sandals and things for me. O Epimetheus, let me have just one look!"

But Epimetheus continued to shake his head and say "No," and Pandora pouted and grew more unhappy and curious all the time.

At last one day when Epimetheus was out, Pandora carefully untied the cord that fastened the lid, then opened the chest. With a buzz and a roar, there flew out a swarm of little, evil-looking, stinging creatures, wildly turning somersaults and leaping with gladness at being free.

They were not pleasant to look at, and Pandora was frightened as she saw them go flying out of the house. In a few moments, Epimetheus came running and shouting with all the men and boys after him, crying out and quarreling and making a dreadful noise.

"Pandora, Pandora!" cried Epimetheus. "You have let loose all the evils and troubles that were in the chest!"

Pandora wept to see Epimetheus so angry. She was sorry that she had ever touched the chest. Epimetheus did not stay to comfort her, but hurried out again and tried to stop the wailing and quarreling.

As Pandora wept and listened to the strange, dreadful sounds outside, a soft hand touched her on the shoulder. She turned quickly and saw a little silvery-white figure, no bigger than the troubles had been, but beautiful and kind looking.

"I am still with you," said the little creature. "You can never be altogether unhappy if I stay; for my name is Hope."

Very gently she flew to Pandora's wrist, and Pandora ran to the door and held her hand high, so that everyone might see. One by one the boys and men looked up and saw the little figure of Hope.

Soon the quarreling and wailing stopped, and ever after, although all the little troubles still flew around the earth, Hope was always somewhere near to help and give comfort.

HERCULES

When Hercules was a baby, he lived in the palace of Amphitryon, king of Thebes. Although Amphitryon loved the baby dearly and provided many women to wait on him and care for him, Hercules was not his own child. He was the son of the great god Jupiter, king of the heavens.

King Amphitryon was proud of him because he was much larger and stronger than other babies, but Juno, who was the wife of Jupiter and queen of all the goddesses, hated this little son of Jupiter.

One day the goddess sent two great serpents to destroy Hercules as he lay in his cradle, but Hercules wakened as the serpents rustled over his linen coverlet; and, reaching out his strong little hands, he grasped them round the neck and held them tight until they were strangled. His nurses, hearing him crow, knew his nap was over, so they came in to take him up. There lay the two serpents dead in his cradle!

This was such a wonderful thing for a baby to do, that King Amphitryon boasted of it all over his kingdom. As Hercules grew older, the king searched far and wide until he found the wisest teachers to train him in all the ways in which a prince should be trained.

Baby Hercules and the serpents

In one way his nurses and teachers had a hard time with Hercules. He had so terrible a temper that when he became angry, everyone ran out of his reach. King Amphitryon tried in many ways to teach Hercules to control his temper, but it was no use. One day his music teacher, whose name was Linus, reproved him for carelessness and tried to punish him. Hercules at once raised his lyre and struck Linus on the head. The blow was such a terrible one that Linus died.

After that Hercules was in disgrace with King Amphitryon, and the king sent him away to live among his herdsmen and the cattle.

In the mountains where the king's herds were kept, there lived a lion which kept carrying off the fattest cows. Often, too, it had killed a herdsman. Soon after Hercules came to live in the mountains, he killed this lion, and in other ways made himself so useful to the herdsmen that they grew to love him, and held him in great respect.

Hercules continued to grow larger and stronger, and at last he returned to Thebes and fought for the king against his enemies. He won many victories for King Amphitryon, who forgave him for killing Linus.

The rest of his life Hercules spent in twelve adventures that were full of danger. Among them was his fight with a terrible lion which lived in the valley of Nemea. When he failed to kill it with his club, he strangled it with his hands, and returned carrying the body of the great beast across his shoulders.

Hercules returned carrying the body of the great beast

Next he killed a nine-headed water serpent called the Hydra, which lived in the country of Argos; and then he captured a boar that had long overrun the mountains of Arcadia, frightening and killing the people.

From one of Hercules' adventures he returned bringing a wonderful stag with antlers of gold and feet of brass, which dwelt in the hills about Arcadia.

Whenever Hercules heard of a monster that preyed on the people, he at once set out to overcome it. Sometimes he was sent on these dangerous adventures by Juno, who still wished that harm might befall him; but Hercules had the help of Jupiter, and each time returned victorious.

He was sent to clean the stables of King Augeas, who had a herd of three thousand oxen, whose stalls had not been cleaned in thirty years. Hercules cleverly thought of a way to clean the filthy stables without even entering them. He dug a wide ditch from a river to the stables, and let the waters rush through the stalls into a ditch on the other side and down the hill into another river. In a few hours the stables were clean. Then Hercules walled up the opening between the first river and the ditch so that no more water could flow through. When King Augeas came to look at his stables, much to his astonishment he found them clean and dry.

The three daughters of Hesperus guarding the golden apples

Hercules was also sent to find the golden apples that were guarded by the three daughters of Hesperus and by a great dragon, which coiled itself among the trees of the garden.

Hercules knew that Atlas owned the gardens of the Hesperides, so he journeyed to the mountain of Atlas and asked him if he would not like to rest from the weight of the sky, which he had held on his great shoulders ever since Perseus turned him into stone.

Hercules offered, with Jupiter's help, to change Atlas back into a giant, so that he might walk the earth and wade in cool streams and rest in green valleys. This he would do if Atlas would agree to go to his garden and gather some golden apples for him. Atlas was eager to be released from the burden of the sky and the stars, and promised to do anything Hercules wished if only he might once more be free.

So Hercules took the weight of the heavens on his own shoulders and Atlas stepped out, shaking his head wildly, shouting and leaping with gladness at being free once more. He went joyously across the land, splashing through cool streams and striding through the green grass.

Hercules held the heavens until Atlas finally returned with his big hands and deep pockets filled with golden apples. Atlas begged that he might carry them to Hercules' land and deliver them. But Hercules was afraid that if Atlas went he might never come back, so he asked Atlas to hold the earth until he rested his shoulders. He then set the sky again on the giant's shoulders and went back to Thebes with the golden apples.

In spite of his temper, Hercules was kind. Learning that Prometheus was still chained to the rock where Jupiter had bound him, he urged his father to give him permission to break the chains that held Prometheus and set him free. Jupiter agreed, and Prometheus, after his long punishment, was unbound.

At last, after many glorious labors, Hercules was carried to Mount Olympus in Jupiter's own chariot, and became one of the Immortals.

Hercules held up the heavens

APOLLO AND DIANA

One day, on an island in the sea of the dawn, a pair of twins, a boy and a girl, were born. Their mother, Latona, named them Apollo and Diana.

Jupiter, the ruler of the gods, was fond of beautiful children, but Juno, his wife, was hard-hearted and liked much better to pet her peacock than to cuddle the dearest baby that ever lived.

Jupiter sent many blessings and gifts to Apollo and Diana and often went down to earth to visit them. This made Juno very angry.

The island on which Apollo and Diana were born was small and rocky, so, aided by Jupiter, their mother crossed the sea of the dawn to another country where there was a fair garden with fruit and wild honey and many other pleasant things for Latona and her children.

Juno, looking down from Olympus, was angry and said, "Jupiter is visiting Apollo and Diana again."

She waited until Jupiter had returned to Mount Olympus, and then hurried down to earth. Changing herself into fierce and dreadful forms, she frightened Latona so that she ran from the beautiful garden Jupiter had found for her. Carrying the twins in her arms, Latona wandered far away through cold and desolate lands.

Juno followed and tormented Latona in many ways. Apollo and Diana were large and heavy to carry. But when Latona grew tired and tried to rest, Juno sent wild animals to howl horribly behind her and insects to sting her, so the poor mother, the twins pressed closely to her bosom, stumbled on, although she was ready to fall from weariness.

Latona wandered far away through desolate lands

At last, footsore and thirsty, she came to a little pond of clear water and thought she might stop to rest and drink. On the shores of the pond a band of country people were cutting willows to make baskets. At once, Juno filled their hearts with unkindness, and, throwing down their knives and willows, they shouted rudely at Latona and bade her be gone.

"Go away from our lake," they said, and threatened to harm her if she did not leave.

"But I am so thirsty," begged Latona.

"Ha, ha," cried the rustics, "then you may drink mud." And as they spoke they waded into the pond, stirring up the mud with sticks and with their feet until the cool waters of the little pond were no longer clear, but brown and dirty.

Latona stood up and, holding her head high in anger, said to the rustics, "Since you like this lake so well you shall stay here forever."

The rustics waded into the pond, stirring up the mud with sticks and their feet

As Latona spoke, the sky grew dark, the lightning flashed, and the thunder rumbled loudly overhead. The men and boys vanished, and their empty tunics floated on the muddy waters of the pond. Here and there above the water peeped the green heads of bullfrogs. Latona in her anger had changed the rustics into frogs.

When Jupiter learned that Latona, with Apollo and Diana, had been driven from the garden, he led them to a lovely mountain on the island of Delos. There Latona dwelt happily in peace and quiet and cared for her children.

Before Apollo was ten years old he left his mother and his twin sister, Diana, and traveled to a fair and distant land, the home of the Hyperboreans, where spring lasted one half of the year and summer the other half.

When Apollo returned to Delos to see his mother and Diana, he came riding over the water in a chariot drawn by white swans. Latona and Diana were glad to see him and were greatly interested in the chariot, which was wreathed with flowers. Apollo told them that Jupiter had given it to him so that he might return to visit them.

Jupiter saw Apollo as he unharnessed the swans from his chariot. His heart was full of pride in the beautiful boy.

"The swan chariot will do for Apollo now," said the ruler of the gods, "but when he is grown, Helios shall rest, and Apollo shall drive the chariot of the sun.

"Instead of white swans I will give him the swift horses of the day. The flowers of the Hyperboreans may wreathe his chariot now, but I will give him a chariot wreathed in fire."

Long ago, Vulcan had made the chariot of the sun and bathed it in fire from his magic forge. Ever after, the chariot flamed and glowed with a light that could not be put out. Hyperion was the first one to drive this wonderful chariot, and the next was Helios, his son. Helios had driven it for so many years that now he was weary and ready to rest.

When Apollo was grown, Jupiter sent for him and showed him the golden chariot.

"You shall harness your white swans no more!" said Jupiter. "Take the sun into your keeping, and drive the chariot of the sun and the four horses of the day!"

Apollo sprang into the chariot, amazed and delighted at its wonderful beauty. Helios showed him the way he must go, and watched the sun rise in the sky and journey toward the west, glad indeed that Apollo was old enough to drive, so that he might rest and give up his journeyings.

That evening, when Apollo had returned his horses to their stables and had hidden his chariot behind banks of purple clouds, he hurried back to his mother and his sister Diana and told them of Jupiter's gift.

Apollo came riding over the water in a chariot drawn by white swans

Apollo and Diana go to Mount Olympus

When Diana heard of the honor that had fallen to her brother, she was both proud and vexed.

"You have journeyed to the land of the Hyperboreans and visited many other places that I have not seen," she said. "While I stayed with our mother and cheered her, you rode in your swan-drawn chariot wherever you wished, and now Jupiter gives you the sun to drive and gives nothing at all to me.

"Tomorrow before dawn, when you go to Mount Olympus, I am going with you. I shall remind Jupiter that I am your twin, and if you light the sky by day with the chariot of Helios, then I must have Thea's silver fire to light the heavens when you rest."

In the morning, Apollo rose early to present himself to Jupiter before driving the chariot. Diana rose also and went with him to Mount Olympus.

Jupiter was much surprised to see the fair twin sister of Apollo, for he had not thought of Diana for a long time. He remembered how lovely she had been when a child, and he saw that now she was even more beautiful.

When Jupiter heard that Diana wished to light the sky at night, he gave the silver orb of the moon into her keeping.

Now, when Apollo has finished his course and hides his lofty chariot behind the evening clouds, Diana enters her carriage and drives her milk-white steeds across the broad pathway of heaven. Then, while her brother sleeps, she lights the earth and sea and heavens with her soft, silvery light.

DAEDALUS AND ICARUS

There was once a boy named Icarus who, with his father, Daedalus, was imprisoned in a tower on the island of Crete.

From the little window of this lonely tower they could see the blue ocean and watch the gulls and eagles sweep back and forth over the island.

Sometimes a ship sailed out toward other lands, and then Daedalus and Icarus would long for freedom, and wish that they might sail away to Delos and never again see the island of Crete.

Daedalus at last found a way for them to escape from the tower, but they were obliged to hide themselves in the loneliest parts of the island. Minos, the king who had put them in prison, watched the coming and going of all ships, and so Daedalus and Icarus never found courage to go near the harbor where the outgoing galleys lay anchored.

In spite of this, Icarus was almost happy. Besides the blue sea, the ships, and the birds, which he loved to watch, he found shellfish along the shore, crabs among the rocks, and many other curious things.

But Daedalus grew more lonely and miserable and spent all his time watching the gulls as they flew in the air, and planning how he and Icarus might escape from the island.

One day Icarus was throwing stones at the gulls. He killed one of the birds and brought it to his father.

Icarus went higher and higher into the heavens

"See how the feathers shine, and how long the wings are!" said the young boy.

Daedalus took the bird in his hands and turned it over slowly, examining the wings.

"See," said Icarus, "how the feathers shine, and how long the wings are!"

"Now, if we had wings," laughed Icarus, "we could fly away and be free."

For a long time his father sat silent, holding the dead bird. Now and then he looked up and watched other birds as they wheeled in the air over the sea and the island.

At last he said softly to himself, "We shall have wings, too."

After that, Daedalus was idle no more. He plucked feathers from all the birds that Icarus could kill and began to make two great wings. He fastened the feathers to a framework with melted wax and threads pulled from his linen cloak.

When these two wings were finished, Daedalus bound them on himself. He rose into the air, waving his arms, now up, now down, and went soaring far out over the water.

Icarus jumped about in delight, and shouted to his father to come back and make another pair of wings so that they might fly away and leave Crete forever.

When Daedalus had finished another pair of wings, he bound the smaller pair on his son. Then he warned Icarus not to wander off alone in the air but to follow him closely.

"If you fly too low, the dampness of the sea will make your feathers heavy, and you will sink into the water," said Daedalus. "But if you fly too near the sun, the heat will melt the wax and you will fall."

Icarus promised to fly just as his father bade him. Leaping from the highest cliff on the island, they flew away toward Delos.

At first Icarus was obedient and followed close behind his father. But soon, in the joy of flying, he forgot all that his father had told him; and, stretching his arms upward, he went higher and higher into the heavens.

Daedalus called to him to return, but the wind passed so swiftly that it carried all sound away, and Icarus could not hear. His wings bore him higher and still higher into the region of the clouds. As he went up and up, the air grew warmer and warmer, but he forgot his father's warning and flew on.

At length Icarus saw feathers floating in the air around him and suddenly he remembered his father's warning. He knew that the heat of the sun had melted the wax that held the feathers to the framework.

Finally Icarus felt himself sinking! He fluttered his wings wildly in an effort to fly, but such a storm of feathers swept around him that he could not see.

With a wild cry, turning and whirling through the sky, poor Icarus fell down into the blue waters of the sea—known ever since as the Icarian.

Daedalus heard his cry and flew to the spot, but nothing could be seen of Icarus or his wings except a handful of white feathers floating on the water.

Sadly the father went on with his journey, and finally reached the shore of a friendly island. There he built a temple to Apollo and hung up his wings as an offering to the god. But ever after he mourned his son, and never again did he try to fly.

JASON AND THE GOLDEN FLEECE

There was once a young prince named Jason. His parents ruled over Iolcus, in Thessaly. Their kingdom was filled with happiness and peace, for they were wise and good and noble.

But one day the King's brother, Pelias, came riding at the head of an army. He made war on Iolcus, and took the kingdom from Jason's father. Pelias had evil in his heart, and would have killed his brother and Prince Jason, but they fled and hid themselves among lowly people who loved them.

Now, there was at this time a strange and wonderful school in the mountains of Thessaly, a school where the princes of Greece were taught and made strong of body and brave of heart.

Chiron the centaur

Chiron, the centaur, kept this school and reared the young princes. He taught them how to hunt and to fight and to sing, how to take care of their bodies and to bear themselves according to their noble birth.

So Jason, being still a little boy, was sent to this wonderful school. Here he grew up with the other Greek princes of his age.

At last came the time when Chiron told him the story of the evil King Pelias, who had stolen the kingdom of Iolcus and had driven Jason's father from his throne.

Jason was brown and strong and hardened by Chiron's training. He girded on his sword and set out to take the kingdom away from Pelias.

It was early in spring, and as Jason journeyed he came to a swollen stream and saw an aged woman gazing in despair at the waters she could not cross.

Jason remembered his training as a prince, and offered to carry her across. He lifted her to his back and she gave him her staff for support. He stepped into the swift-running stream, which no one else had dared cross; and although he bent under the weight of his burden, he fought bravely against the waters with all his strength.

At last he reached the opposite bank and set the old woman on the grass. Suddenly, in a flash of light, she was transformed into the glorious figure of Juno, queen of the gods. At her feet stood a peacock. Its purple and blue and green tail feathers swept over the grass, and its shining head rested against her hand.

The goddess promised aid and protection to Jason forever after, and vanished as quickly as she had appeared. So in all his undertakings Jason was watched over and blessed by Juno in return for his kindness to her.

At last Jason reached Iolcus and demanded the throne from Pelias. That crafty and wicked old King did not refuse him at once. A banquet was prepared, and with every appearance of kindness, King Pelias did honor to young Jason. The King feasted him and seemed to welcome him to Iolcus, but in reality he planned Jason's death.

While they ate, the bards gathered around the hall and sang of heroes and brave deeds, as bards were accustomed to sing at banquets of kings.

The ram leapt into the air and flew through the clouds as if he had wings

They sang of the story of Phrixus and Helle, the two Greek children who escaped from their wicked stepmother, riding on the back of Mercury's golden-fleeced ram. They sang of how Nephele, the real mother, weeping and heavy of heart, placed her little son and daughter on the ram's back and watched them as they sped away from Thessaly. The ram leapt into the air and flew through the clouds as if he had wings. They passed over the sea toward Colchis, the kingdom of their uncle, where they knew they would be safe.

The bards touched their lyre strings sadly and sang of how little Helle became frightened as she looked down upon the tossing sea, and how she fell from the ram's back into the water, which ever after was called Hellespont.

But Phrixus clung fast and reached Colchis in safety. He offered the ram as an offering of thanks to the gods, and hung the Golden Fleece high on an oak tree, setting a fearful dragon to guard it. Here after all the years it still hung, waiting for some young hero to conquer and claim it.

The bards sang of the glory of the Fleece, of its glittering richness, and of the heroes who had died seeking it. Pelias noticed how Jason's eyes were shining. He knew that the song had moved him and rightly guessed that Jason longed to go in search of this Golden Fleece.

Pelias thought that this would be a good way to bring about Jason's death. The dragon had killed many other youths who had been rash enough to seek the Golden Fleece, and Pelias felt certain that Jason would perish also. So he leaned toward the young prince and urged him to set out on the adventure and bring back the Fleece which rightfully belonged to Thessaly.

Jason sprang from his seat and vowed that he would go. First he visited Juno's temple and asked for help on his journey. She gave him the limb of a mighty and wonderful oak for the figurehead of his boat; the branch would speak to him in time of danger, and advise and warn him on his voyage.

Then Juno bade Minerva provide a swift-sailing vessel, made from the wood of pine trees which grew on Mount Pelion.

Jason called his vessel the *Argo*, and sent for the young princes of Chiron's school to come with him and help in the search for the Golden Fleece.

Juno sped them on their way with favorable winds

Medea was skilled in all manner of enchantments and magic

Hercules came and also Admetus, Theseus, Orpheus, Castor and Pollux: all the bravest and noblest heroes of Greece, anxious to take part in this adventure and to bring the Golden Fleece back to Thessaly.

Juno sped them on their way with favorable winds, and the *Argo* sailed swiftly toward Colchis. When danger threatened, the branch of the talking oak spoke wise words of help and counsel. It guided them safely between the clashing rocks of the Symplegades, and past the land of the cruel Harpies. So they came at last, after many adventures, to Colchis, the kingdom of Eetes.

Now, the Fleece had hung for so long in his realm that King Eetes was unwilling to part with it. Like Pelias, he was crafty and full of wiles, and did not refuse Jason, but agreed to give him the Fleece on certain conditions.

First Jason must catch and harness two wild fire-breathing bulls, then plow a stony field, sacred to Mars. After that he must sow the field with dragon's teeth and conquer the host of armed men that would grow from them. Last of all, he must overcome the dragon which coiled around the foot of the oak and guarded the Fleece.

Jason and the fiery bulls

Jason feared that these tasks were impossible for any mortal to fulfill without the help of the gods. So he hurried down to the vessel to speak with the branch of the talking oak. On his way he met Medea, the princess of Colchis. She was young and beautiful and skilled in all manner of enchantments and magic. Her heart was filled with kindness toward the brave young stranger and she wished to help him.

She gave Jason her strongest charms and her wisest counsel. By the aid of Medea's magic, he caught the fiery bulls as they came roaring from their pasture. He harnessed them and drove them over the stony field, and made them drag a heavy plow that turned the earth in dark furrows.

Eetes was amazed, for no one had ever yoked or harnessed these bulls before.

When the field was ready, Jason asked for the dragon's teeth, and Eetes gave them to him in a helmet. Up and down the long furrows he sowed them, and when the last one was in the ground, he plowed the earth again, and covered them and waited.

Long rows of shining spears began to pierce the ground and to shoot up into the air. Then rose the plumed helmets of a thousand soldiers; then their shields and their bodies.

They stood, full-armed and fierce, looking over the field. When they beheld Jason, they ran toward him with waving spears and a clatter of shields.

Because she loved him, Medea left her father's land and sailed away in the *Argo* with Jason and his comrades.

But, sad to relate, they did not live happily ever after, for Medea knew so much sorcery that she was forever practicing new magic and often she brought trouble on herself and Jason.

On the way back to Thessaly they passed through many dangers, but at last, with Juno's help, came safely home.

Jason and his comrades forced the evil King Pelias to give back the throne. Once more the people of Thessaly lived in happiness and peace under the rule of their own rightful king.

THE GOLDEN TOUCH

There was once a very rich king named Midas. The columns of his palace were inlaid with gold, and his treasure room was filled with jewels, yet he was not satisfied. He longed for greater wealth. He did not care for music or flowers, or indeed for anything else except his beautiful little daughter and his riches.

Midas wished to give his daughter, Marigold, the finest dresses ever made, the most beautiful beads and jeweled bands for her hair. This was one reason why he longed to have more gold and riches. But Marigold loved to wear a short white frock, and to go barefoot over the grass with only a band of ribbon on her head.

She liked to feel the cool wind blow through her curls; she loved roses and violets much better than jewels. Sometimes she begged King Midas to leave his treasure room, where he liked to sit, to walk in the woods with her.

"The birds are singing," she would say, "and the very first flowers are in bloom."

But Midas would pat her head and tell her to run out and play—just as all busy fathers have told their little girls ever since.

One day, as Midas sat counting his riches, a stranger walked into the room and touched him on the shoulder. Vines twined around the visitor's head, and a leopard skin hung from his shoulders.

Marigold, the little daughter of King Midas

"Who are you?" cried Midas in alarm, "and how did you pass the guards?"

"I am Bacchus," said the stranger. "I have come to thank you. Not long ago you were kind to my old teacher, Silenus. The gods do not forget such things."

Then Midas remembered that one evening an aged man had stumbled into the palace. Midas had given him shelter and food and fresh clothing. In the morning the King had sent him on his way with a companion to guide him.

Midas rose to his feet—as even a royal mortal should stand in the presence of the gods—and bowed low to Bacchus, inviting him to be seated. Bacchus looked at the chair inlaid with gold. He saw the table strewn with jewels and coins and glittering bowls. He shuddered and moved farther away from Midas.

"I cannot stay in this room," said Bacchus. "There is no sunshine here, nor any sound of the wind in the vine leaves."

Midas looked at the god in amazement.

"You talk like my daughter, Marigold," said he. "True, there is no sunshine here, but look! See the golden lights on these bowls, and the red glow on the jewels!"

"Have you seen the colors of grapes when the sun shines through them, purple and red and amber?" asked Bacchus.

"No," said Midas, "I like grapes only when they are brought to me on a golden platter. There is nothing in the world so lovely as gold. I wish that everything I touch might be changed into that beautiful metal. Then I should be happy."

"You shall have your wish," said Bacchus, hurrying away out of the gloomy room to his vineyards on the sunny hills.

"I shall have my wish!" whispered Midas delightedly. "Can he really mean it?"

Just then the palace servants struck the big gong and called the King to dinner.

Midas locked the door of his treasury and walked toward the room where his dinner awaited him. He glanced down at the great key in his hand. It was gold! His sleeve, too, gleamed a dull yellow and felt stiff to his touch. His belt was changed into the same metal. His sandals and everything he wore were shining gold.

He touched a marble column as he passed, and it turned yellow. The curtains which he brushed in passing grew rigid and gleaming.

Marigold came dancing in from the woods, her hands full of white flowers. She sat down in her tall chair beside the King's.

"Why, Father," she said, "when did you buy that funny stiff robe? And your yellow sandals, where did you get them?"

Midas smiled delightedly as he sat down. "They are solid gold, my dear! The gods have given me the Golden Touch. You may have anything in the world that you wish."

"Look at your chair, Father!" cried Marigold.

"No doubt it also is gold," smiled Midas, turning to see. "It seems more comfortable than ever. I shall have every chair in the palace made over."

He took his white napkin in his hand and shook it out. It was wonderful to see the golden color spread over the snowy linen, almost as if a yellow flame ran up the folds.

Smiling broadly, he reached for his spoon. "We shall have all the golden dishes we like," he said.

Then he raised a spoonful of the savory soup to his mouth. He tasted it, and it was very good. But oh, horrible! When he tried to swallow it, the taste vanished and there was nothing in his mouth but a hard lump. He choked and sputtered and coughed.

He looked at his plate in surprise.

"Can there be a stone in my soup?" he wondered.

Midas tried another spoonful, but the same thing happened. He broke a piece of white bread, and it turned to gold as he raised it to his lips. He touched an apple and a pear. They became hard and glittering.

"Oh!" shouted the King, "I do not want my food to become gold. Everything else, O great god Bacchus, but not my food!"

Bacchus did not hear. He was far away in his vineyards listening to Pan's music. Marigold climbed down from her tall chair, and ran to the King.

"O dear Father," she said, "what has happened?" She put her arms around his neck and her cheek to his. At the same moment her skin grew dark and yellow. The pink and white of her cheek vanished. Only her hair remained its own color, for her curls had always been like spun gold.

Midas put his hand on her to caress her, then drew away in terror. For his little daughter was now cold and hard, a golden statue.

"O Bacchus, O great Bacchus!" cried Midas, leaping to his feet, "take away this dreadful gift. My daughter has become a golden image. Everything I touch grows hard and cold. Give me back my little girl, or let me die!"

Bacchus heard at last, and came down from the hilltop and entered the palace.

"Well, Midas," he asked, "do you still care so much for gold?"

"No, no!" said the King. "Take away the Golden Touch and give me my Marigold."

Bacchus smiled wisely at the King.

"Perhaps now you will like the sunshine as much as gold," said the god, "and the glowing lights in grapes better than the glitter of stones. Perhaps now you will leave your treasure room sometimes and walk in the woods with Marigold."

"I will, I will!" promised Midas. "Only let her live again!"

"Then go to the river and wash," said Bacchus.

"O great Bacchus," cried Midas, "take away this dreadful gift"

Midas splashed into the river

Midas ran as fast as he could out of the room and down the marble steps, which turned to gold as he passed. In the garden, the rose bushes which he brushed lost their green color and became tawny yellow. The gravel path changed, and the grass where he walked showed his footprints in yellow tracks.

Down the riverbank Midas stumbled, and splashed into the water.

His garments became soft and white. His belt and sandals were of leather once more. But the river sands where he washed became golden, and remained so forever.

He ran back to the palace and took the golden figure of little Marigold in his arms. At first she felt hard and cold to his touch, but in a moment Marigold's arms moved, her color returned, and she grew soft and warm.

"Oh, Father," she said, "I had a strange dream. I dreamed that I could not speak, or move, or—"

"Never mind, my sweetheart," said the King, "that is all over."

"And I dreamed that your robe was made of gold—"

"But see, it is soft white linen now," said Midas. "Let us eat."

The servants brought more hot food, and Midas and his daughter finished their dinner. Never had soup tasted so good to him, nor fruit so juicy. His napkin seemed more beautiful in its snowy whiteness than any golden fabric he had ever seen.

When they rose from the table, Marigold showed him the delicate white flowers.

"There are whole banks of them in the woods," she said. "And when the sun shines on them, and the wind blows, they look just like little dancing nymphs with yellow hair and white tunics. Won't you come with me and see them?"

"Indeed, yes," said Midas.

He put his hand in Marigold's and walked with her to the woods. There he found more happiness than he had ever known in his treasure room, and learned to love the white buds of flowers more than the largest pearls in his treasure chests.

CUPID AND APOLLO

Cupid was the baby son of Venus. Although his mother fed him daily with nectar and ambrosia, the food of the gods, he never seemed to grow. The years passed by, and still Cupid remained a tiny, dimpled, laughing child, although he could fly and run wherever he wished and care for himself on earth as well as on Mount Olympus.

When Apollo was not driving his chariot, Cupid loved to follow him around, for he was more fond of Apollo than of any of the other gods. He was much interested in Apollo's bow and arrows and longed to take them in his hand.

Once he saw Apollo take his strongest bow and his sharpest arrows and set out to kill a huge, dark monster called the Python.

The Python was a gloomy creature that breathed heavy black smoke from his nostrils. This filled the air for miles around with darkness, and the shadows were so heavy that no one standing in the valley could see the mountaintops.

As Apollo was the god of light, he did not like the darkness, so he went straight into the shadowy valley, found the terrible Python, and then killed him.

Cupid followed him so quietly that Apollo did not know he was there until after the Python was killed, and the darkness had lifted from the valley. Then he saw the boy standing beside him.

"Oh, your arrows are wonderful!" cried Cupid. "Give me one! I'll do anything you say if you will only let me hold your bow."

But Apollo laughed; and taking Cupid's hand in his, led him back to his mother.

Cupid, the baby son of Venus

Cupid was greatly disappointed and decided that if he could not have Apollo's bow and arrows he would get some for himself. He knew that almost anything he wished for, Vulcan could make at his anvil; and so one day he asked for a bow like Apollo's, and a quiver of golden arrows.

Vulcan fashioned a little bow, perfect and smooth and slender, and a quiver full of the sharpest, lightest arrows.

"What have you to do with warlike weapons, saucy boy?"

Venus, who was watching, gave to these darts a power no large arrows had ever possessed. When anyone was touched ever so lightly by one of these golden arrows, he at once fell in love with the first person he saw.

Cupid was so delighted with his bow and arrows that he played with them from morning until night.

One day Apollo did not drive his chariot, but left it in the heavens behind the clouds.

"It is a good thing," he said, "for people to have some gray days." So he spent the day hunting through the forest.

In a little glade he came upon Cupid sitting on a mossy rock, playing with his bow and arrows. Apollo was much vexed to think that Cupid could handle so cleverly the same kind of weapons that he had used to kill the Python. He frowned, and spoke harshly to him.

"What have you to do with warlike weapons, saucy boy?" said Apollo. "Put them down and leave such things for grown people."

Cupid was hurt and angry. He had hoped Apollo would praise him for his skill, as Venus had done.

"Your arrows may kill the Python," said Cupid, "but mine shall wound *you*."

As he spoke he let fly an arrow, which struck Apollo so lightly it barely scratched him. Apollo laughed at him and walked on, not knowing what the wound really meant.

Daphne was so shy she ran away

Soon he noticed a beautiful nymph gathering flowers in the forest. Her name was Daphne. Apollo had often seen her before, but she had never seemed so beautiful as now. He ran forward to speak to her. She saw him coming and was startled.

"Let me help you gather flowers," begged Apollo, but Daphne was so shy she ran away. Apollo wanted so much to be with her and talk to her that he ran after her.

Poor Daphne, terrified, ran faster and faster. When she was breathless and could run no more, she cried to Peneus the river god for help.

Peneus was her father, and, hearing his daughter's voice from far away, he thought she was in some terrible danger. Swiftly he sent his magic power over the forest, and to protect her, changed her into a tree.

Daphne's feet clung to the earth and took root. She felt the rough bark creeping over her shoulders and limbs. From her arms sprang branches, and her hands were filled with leaves. When Apollo reached out his hand to touch her, the fair maiden had vanished. In her place stood a beautiful laurel tree.

"What have I done?" mourned Apollo.

He was so grieved and sad because he had brought this change on Daphne that he stayed by the tree all the afternoon, talking to it and begging Daphne to forgive him.

He asked for some of her laurel leaves that he might wear them on his head. Daphne shook her branches, and a little shower of leaves fell around Apollo. By this he knew that Daphne forgave him, and he gathered the leaves tenderly in his hands and wove them into a wreath.

Throwing aside a drooping wreath of flowers which he wore about his brow, Apollo placed the laurel on his head, where it remained forever fresh and green.

PROSERPINA AND PLUTO

Pluto was god of Erebus, the world that lies beneath the ground. In his realm, all was dark, misty, and gloomy. There was no sunshine there, nor any light except the glow of fires. Instead of blue sky overhead, he had only a roof of damp and dripping earth. There were no bright-colored flowers in his kingdom, nor tall branching trees, nor green grass.

In some places the dripping water mingled with rust-colored lime from the earth, and hardened into all sorts of shapes. It made columns and arches and mounds, or hung like icicles in long, thin pendants from the roofs of Pluto's many caverns. There were black marble rocks in Erebus, and deep, dark lakes.

It would have been a dreary place for an earth child, but Pluto thought his kingdom the most beautiful in the world. He thought his caves hung with lime crystals far lovelier than forests of birch trees. He liked the noiseless peace of the dim caverns. No songs of birds nor rustle of wind among the trees disturbed their quiet. Only at times he heard far off the barking of Cerberus, who guarded the entrance to his kingdom.

Pluto seized Proserpina by the wrist

To drive away the dampness in the caves, Pluto lit many fires. Their flickering flames made the lime crystals sparkle and glimmer on the dark waters of the lakes. These fires were silent, too. They never crackled cheerfully as earth fires do.

Pluto, the god of this strange, quiet land,
was content to stay in his own kingdom

The god of this strange, quiet land was content to stay in his own kingdom and seldom journeyed to the earth, which seemed a noisy place after the deep silence of Erebus.

But once Jupiter imprisoned four great giants in a cavern in Mount Aetna. In their anger, the giants stamped their feet and shook the earth, raging back and forth and beating on the walls of their prison, or heaving their mighty shoulders against the sides of the cavern until the mountain trembled.

Far off in his kingdom under the ground, Pluto heard these strange rumblings and feared that the surface of the earth might crack from the shock and the light of day break through.

So, mounting his chariot drawn by four black horses, Pluto journeyed swiftly up to earth and rode here and there to see how much damage had been done by the angry giants.

He found temples overturned, trees uprooted, and rocks thrown about as though some great earthquake had shaken the land, but no cracks deep enough to disturb the gloom of Erebus.

Pluto was preparing to return home, for the light of the sun was painful to his eyes, and he did not like the strange perfume of the earth-flowers nor the sound of wind in the trees. But Cupid, that mischievous god of love, had other plans for Pluto.

He drew his bow, wounding the god of darkness with one of those arrows that cause the wounded one to love the first person he meets.

Pluto had just grasped the reins of his four black horses to turn them homeward, when he saw Proserpina, the daughter of the goddess Ceres, with half a dozen nymphs, dancing across the valley. Proserpina's hair floated behind her, bright as a flame of golden fire, and her eyes were as black as Pluto's lakes. She came nearer, gathering flowers and twining them into garlands.

The god of the dark kingdom stepped from his chariot and left it hidden among the trees. His cloak waved about him in many points and folds, thin and fluttering like a garment of smoke. Little tongues of fire rose from his crown and flickered above his forehead.

Proserpina and the nymphs saw him and drew back in alarm. Pluto strode toward them and seized Proserpina by the wrist. He did not woo her gently and kindly as suitors do. He said nothing at all, but lifted her in his arms and carried her off into the forest. Stepping into his chariot, Pluto seized the reins with one hand, and held Proserpina with the other. The four black horses sprang forward with a bound, galloping madly away toward the River Cyane.

Proserpina screamed for help. She cried to Ceres, her mother, but Pluto urged on his horses, and the chariot dashed away still faster.

When they reached the edge of the River Cyane, Pluto commanded the waters to open so that he might pass, but the river nymph saw that Proserpina was being carried away, and refused to help Pluto or make a pathway for him to cross.

Then, in anger, Pluto struck the ground with his mighty three-pronged spear, and the earth itself opened. The horses plunged downward, and with the chariot rattling from side to side, disappeared into the darkness.

Now, far off, Ceres had heard Proserpina's cry as Pluto carried her away. A sharp pain shot through the mother's heart, and like a bird she flew through forest and valley, seeking Proserpina. She climbed mountains and crossed rivers, asking everyone she met for tidings of Proserpina, but neither man nor god would tell her where Pluto had carried her daughter.

A long, dark cloak hid the brightness of Ceres' hair

A long, dark cloak hid Ceres' face and the brightness of her hair. No one who saw her then would have known that she was the glowing goddess of the harvest. For many days she wandered over the earth, refusing in her sorrow to taste either ambrosia or nectar.

Once, as she sat on a stone resting beside a well, the four daughters of Celeus, running and leaping like young gazelles, came to fill their pitchers.

They saw the aged woman at the spring. Her head was bent in sorrow, and her dark cloak spoke of mourning. They touched her gently on the

*The four daughters of Celeus, running and leaping like young gazelles,
came to fill their pitchers at the well*

shoulder and asked her why she grieved, but Ceres did not tell them
or let them know that she was a goddess. She let them think she was only
an aged woman in trouble.

When their pitchers were filled, they put their arms around Ceres and
led her home. Everyone in the house of Celeus was so gentle and kind
that Ceres found comfort in her sorrow.

Celeus had an infant son who fell ill while Ceres rested in his home.
The goddess nursed the little boy and gave him heavenly gifts, so that he
grew in strength and beauty and wisdom.

Celeus and his family begged the visitor to live with them always, but Ceres wandered on, still seeking Proserpina.

The nymphs shivered and wrapped their robes around them

At last she came to the banks of the River Cyane, but the river nymph, fearing the anger of Pluto, dared not tell Ceres where the missing Proserpina was hidden.

Now, it happened that as Pluto's horses had dashed down into the earth, Proserpina's belt, loosened by her struggle to free herself, fell from the chariot and lay on the riverbank.

The river nymph now took this belt and floated it to where Ceres stood mourning at the water's edge.

Ceres saw it, and now her grief was more terrible than ever. She took away her blessing from the earth and cast an evil spell on all the fruits and crops.

The leaves of the trees lost their green and began to fall in clouds of yellow. The blue sky grew angry and gray, and a cold wind swept over the earth. The nymphs shivered and wrapped their thin robes around them.

Everything became dry and withered, and famine and sickness and grief were over the whole earth.

Then the fountain, Arethusa, spoke to Ceres and told her where Proserpina was. "I come from far down in the earth," sang the fountain. "My waters have trickled through the realms of Pluto. I have seen your daughter. I have seen Proserpina, the beautiful, the bright, sitting on a black marble throne, queen of the spirits which wander silently between the crystal pillars and the flickering fires, and float over the lakes from which my waters rise."

When Ceres heard this, she raised her arms to Jupiter and begged him to return Proserpina to the earth.

"Never again," she cried, "will I make the corn grow or the ripening grain bend in golden waves. Unless my daughter is restored to me, never again will I watch over the harvest. The fruits of the earth shall remain withered, and man shall die from hunger."

Mercury, the speedy messenger of the gods, flew to Pluto

Jupiter feared that Ceres would do as she threatened, so he sent Mercury, the speedy messenger, to fly swiftly to Pluto, and bid him release Proserpina.

"But if she has eaten in Erebus, even I cannot take her from Pluto," said Jupiter.

When Mercury went down into the kingdom of darkness, he took Spring with him. They flew over the River Styx and passed Cerberus, the three-headed dog. When Cerberus, his three great jaws wide open, sprang at them, Spring loosed her cloak and shook such a shower of white petals in his face that he could not see. His mouths were filled with them, and they clung to the lashes of his eyes. Some fell into the River Styx and floated on the dark water.

"They are like the fair queen, Proserpina, on her black marble throne," said Charon, the boatman.

"Such a dreary place for the daughter of Ceres!" thought Mercury, as they flew through the gloomy passages toward Pluto's palace.

Soon Pluto began to notice a faint fragrance that reminded him of the earth world above. He frowned, and hurried to the doors of his palace. Proserpina felt the mild warmth and followed.

They saw Mercury approaching, with Spring floating at his side. "Rejoice, O daughter of Ceres," said Mercury, "for Jupiter bids you return to earth, which lies brown and barren because of grief over your loss."

Pluto frowned more fiercely than ever. "She has eaten six seeds of a pomegranate," he said. "The fates decree that whoever eats in Erebus never may leave."

"Only six little seeds!" begged Proserpina. "There are twice six months in the year. Only let me see my mother! Let me feel the warm sun and soft winds and gather flowers again, and I will come back to you!"

Pluto had grown to love Proserpina dearly. He could not bear to lose her forever, yet he wished her to be happy. So he agreed to let her go back to her mother for six months of the year, but the other six she promised to spend with him.

With Spring on one side and Mercury on the other, Proserpina journeyed up to earth, where Ceres awaited her.

"Proserpina has eaten six seeds of a pomegranate"

As the ground opened to let them out, the cold winds hurried away beyond the sea. Ceres dropped her cloak of gray and laughed with joy to hold her daughter once more in her arms. The bare branches burst into bud, and tiny leaves sprang from every twig. Starry white flowers sprinkled the moss, and the perfume of Spring filled the forest as she began her journey over the earth to star the fields with blossoms and carry the tidings that Proserpina had come back.

PERSEUS and ANDROMEDA

A fisherman was tending his nets one morning on the coast of Seriphus when he noticed something floating far out on the water. He rowed out and found a great wooden chest, which he towed to shore. When the fisherman pried up the heavy cover, he found inside the chest a beautiful princess with a little baby clasped in her arms.

A fisherman was tending his nets on the coast of Seriphus

The fisherman found inside the chest a beautiful princess with a little baby clasped in her arms

She had been shut in the chest for so many hours, floating over the sea, that she was too weak to stand. So the fisherman lifted both baby and mother in his arms and carried them to the King.

Everyone in the palace was greatly surprised to see the strange princess and her baby. King Polydectes ordered food and wine for the mother, and the women of the palace bathed the baby and clothed him in fresh linen.

When the princess had eaten and felt refreshed, she told the King that her name was Danae and that her baby was Perseus, the little son of

Jupiter. She told him that her father, King Acrisius of Argos, had shut them in the chest and set them afloat on the sea because he had heard from an oracle that someday the baby Perseus would grow up and cause his death.

Polydectes was delighted to have Danae stay in the palace, and for a long time he took care of her and her little son. But as Perseus grew up, Polydectes cared less for him, and finally began to wish that Perseus would go away.

So Polydectes sent him on a dangerous journey, to kill the gorgon Medusa, whose cavern was far away in the wilderness. Medusa's head was so terrible to see that no one could look at her without being turned into stone from sheer horror.

Perseus was glad to be sent on this adventure. He armed himself well and set out bravely toward the wilderness where Medusa dwelt.

Minerva, the goddess who watches over heroes, saw him depart, and feared that he could not succeed without the help of the gods. Perseus wore a sword and carried a shield, and his sandals were light and strong; but Minerva knew that he would need weapons and armor more powerful than mortal sword or shield, and sandals swifter than his leather ones.

Therefore she called upon Mercury, who brought his winged sandals of silver. Pluto, god of Erebus, lent his plumed helmet, which would make the wearer invisible. Minerva, herself, gave her shield, which nothing could pierce or shatter.

When Perseus strapped the winged sandals on his feet, he felt himself rise with a strange lightness. When the helmet touched his head,

Mercury brought his winged sandals, Pluto lent his plumed helmet,
amd Minerva herself gave her shield

he became invisible. With the strong and beautiful shield in his hand he set out, as swiftly as Mercury himself, flying through the air over treetops and temples, toward the cavern of the Graeae—the Three Gray Ones.

He knew that these three aged sisters, the Graeae, were exceedingly wise, as wise as they were old, and that if they wished they could tell him where to find Medusa.

As he drew near their cavern, he could hear them singing a mournful song, and, as he peered into the gloomy depths, he saw them rocking back and forth as they sang. They were bent and wrinkled and blind, except for one movable eye which they shared among them. They passed it back and forth as each took her turn at seeing. Their long white hair hung wild and loose on their shoulders.

As Perseus watched, one of them plucked the eye from her forehead and passed it to the sister next to her. For a moment she groped, reaching out for her sister's hand. Instantly, when all the Graeae were in darkness, Perseus sprang into the cavern and snatched the eye as it passed between their fingers.

For a moment there was terrible confusion, for each sister thought one of the others was hiding it. Then Perseus spoke to them and they knew that a stranger had stolen their eye. They stumbled around the cavern, blindly holding out their hands to find him, wailing and pleading all the time.

Perseus was sorry for them, but he did not intend to return their eye until they told him where to find the Gorgon. The Graeae were willing to do anything to have their eye again, and so they agreed to give Perseus all the help they could. They told him exactly in which direction he must go, and just how to find the cavern of Medusa.

Perseus returned their eye and thanked them. Then, swiftly, he flew to the home of Medusa.

Perseus found the entrance to her cave exactly where the Graeae had told him. On every side stood figures of stone, their faces turned toward the cavern. They wore such an expression of terror that Perseus was careful to keep his face turned away, lest he should see Medusa.

Medusa's head was terrible to see

From inside the cave he could hear strange noises, as of someone walking about and complaining. He heard the whispering sound made by the hissing of the serpents which formed Medusa's hair.

Hiding himself behind one of the stone images, he waited until nightfall, then stole up quietly and found the spot where Medusa slept.

Although he kept his head turned aside, he could see her reflection in the brightness of his shield.

Bending over, Perseus cut off the Gorgon's head. Carrying it with him, he hurried to the entrance of the cave. He rose into the air, and flew over the sea and over Africa. As he passed, some drops of the Gorgon's blood fell on the sands of the African desert and immediately changed into poisonous serpents.

At length Perseus came to the realm of a king named Atlas. When he asked for food and rest, Atlas refused him and drove him from the palace doors.

Perseus uncovered the head of Medusa and raised it in front of Atlas. As soon as the King beheld it, he was turned to stone. As Perseus watched, Atlas grew larger and larger. His hips formed the slopes of a mighty mountain; his hair and beard became forests, and thrusting his head high among the stars, he was forced to receive the weight of the sky on his shoulders. Forever after he was doomed to bear that burden.

Perseus flew on until he came to the land of Ethiopia. Here he noticed a group of people on the shore, wringing their hands and weeping. He looked up and saw, chained to a nearby rock, a maiden who kept her face turned toward the sea. She seemed to be expecting something to approach from across the water.

Perseus floated down and, as he came near her, he found that she was the loveliest maiden he had ever beheld. He took off his invisible helmet and spoke to her thus:

"O Maiden undeserving of those chains, tell me, I beseech you, your name and the name of your country, and why you are thus bound."

Replying, the maiden told Perseus that she was Andromeda, Princess of Ethiopia. She was bound to the rock to await the coming of a sea-dragon which would devour her because the gods of the sea were angry with her mother.

Being beautiful and proud of her charms, the Queen of Ethiopia had boasted that she was lovelier than the sea nymphs. Neptune's daughters were angry at this boast, and as a punishment they sent a dreadful sea-dragon to carry off the fairest youths and maidens that lived in the land.

At last the King and Queen were warned by the gods that they must chain their own daughter to a rock so that the dragon might be given the loveliest maiden in all the kingdom. Then, said the oracle, the dragon would he satisfied and would return to the depths of the sea from which he had come.

Even as Andromeda was telling these things to Perseus, they heard a roaring sound that came from the sea. As they looked up, a huge green monster swam swiftly across the water, throwing great fountains of spray toward the heavens.

Perseus sprang into the air. As the dragon came near, he darted downward like an eagle and buried his sword in the serpent's shoulder. Such a fight followed that Andromeda covered her eyes in terror.

The monster lashed his tail to the right and to the left, and in his fury split great rocks. Again and again Perseus rose into the air and swooped down upon him, wounding him until at last he lay still, partly in the water and partly on shore, his head and body stretched on the rocks and the sand, his tail floating far out on the sea.

Perseus unbound the Princess, and the King and Queen gave a great banquet in his honor. Then they allowed him to marry Andromeda and carry her back to his own land.

Perseus returned the helmet to Pluto, the shield to Minerva, and the winged sandals to Mercury, and forever after lived happily with Andromeda.

The oracle which declared that Perseus would cause the death of King Acrisius spoke truly. For one day, after Perseus had returned to his own land, he was playing with the discus and threw it in a course too curved. With a flash of light like that of a swinging sword, the sharp discus flew beyond the limits of the field and struck the King a mortal blow. Thus the words of the ancient oracle came true.

As the dragon came near, Perseus darted downward like an eagle

ATALANTA AND HIPPOMENES

Atalanta was a Greek maiden who could run faster than anyone on earth. She could outrun the winds, Boreas and Zephyr. Only Mercury, with his winged sandals, ran more swiftly.

Besides being so fleet-footed, Atalanta was very beautiful, and many Greek youths from every part of the kingdom wished to marry her. But Atalanta did not wish to marry anyone and turned them all away, saying, "I shall be the bride only of him who shall outrun me in the race, but death must be the penalty of all who try and fail."

In spite of this hard condition, there still were a few brave suitors willing to risk their lives for a chance of winning Atalanta.

For one of the races the runners chose the youth Hippomenes for judge.

Hippomenes felt both pity and scorn for the runners. He thought they were foolish to risk their lives, and bade them go home. He reminded them that the land was full of lovely maidens who were kinder and more gentle than Atalanta.

"But you have not yet seen Atalanta," said one of the suitors to Hippomenes. "You do not know all her beauty and loveliness. See, she comes!"

Hippomenes

Hippomenes looked, and saw Atalanta as she drew near. She laid aside her cloak and made ready for the race. For a moment she stood poised like a graceful white bird about to fly.

The suitors who stood beside her trembled with fear and eagerness.

At a word from Hippomenes, the runners were off; but at the first step Atalanta flew ahead. Her tunic fluttered behind her like a banner. Her hair, loosened from its ribbon, blew about her shoulders in bright waves.

As she ran, Hippomenes thought her very beautiful and became envious of the runner who might win her. He shouted praises when she reached the goal far ahead of her poor suitors.

Hippomenes forgot that the penalty of failure was death. He did not remember the advice he had given the other runners: to go home and forget the loveliness of Atalanta. He knew only that he loved her and must himself race with her.

Raising his head toward Mount Olympus, he prayed to Venus, the goddess of love, and asked her to help him.

As he stood beside Atalanta, waiting the signal for the race to start, Venus appeared to him and slipped three golden apples into his hands.

"Throw them one by one in Atalanta's path," whispered Venus.

The goddess was invisible to everyone but Hippomenes. No one saw Venus as she gave him the apples, nor heard her as she told him what to do with them.

Atalanta looked pityingly at the handsome youth as he stood ready to run. She was sorry for him, and for a moment she hesitated and almost wished that he might win the race.

The signal was given, and Atalanta and Hippomenes flew swiftly over the sand. Atalanta was soon ahead, but Hippomenes, sending up a prayer to Venus, tossed one of his golden apples so that it fell directly in front of Atalanta.

Astonished at the beautiful apple which seemed to fall from nowhere, she stooped to pick it up.

That instant Hippomenes passed her, but Atalanta, holding the apple firmly in her hand, at once darted ahead. Again she outdistanced Hippomenes. Then he threw the second apple.

Atalanta could not pass without picking it up, and then, because of the apple in her other hand, paused a moment longer.

Atalanta stooped to pick up the golden apple

When she looked up, Hippomenes was far ahead.

But, gaining, she overtook and passed him. Then, just before she reached the goal, he threw the third apple.

"I can win easily," thought Atalanta, "even though I stoop for this other apple." As she was already holding an apple in each hand, she paused just for an instant as she wondered how to grasp the third.

At that moment, Hippomenes suddenly shot past, reaching the goal before Atalanta.

Amid the wild shouts of those who watched, he wrapped the maiden's cloak around her shoulders and led her away. Hippomenes was so happy that he forgot to thank the goddess Venus, who followed them to the marriage feast.

Invisible, she moved among the wedding guests. She saw Atalanta place the golden apples in a bowl of ivory and admire their beauty, but Hippomenes, in his delight, thought no more of the apples or of the goddess who had given them to him.

Venus was angry with Hippomenes for being so thoughtless, and instead of blessing the couple, she caused them to be changed into a lion and a lioness, doomed forever to draw the chariot of Cybele, the mother of Jupiter, through the heavens and over the earth.